THIS BOOK BELONGS TO:

CONTACT INFORMATION
NAME
ADDRESS
PHONE #
EMAIL

Copyright © Teresa Rother
All rights reserved. No part of this publication may be reproduced, distributed, or transmitted in any form or by any means, including photocopy, recording, or other electronic or mechanical methods.

DEDICATION

This Reseller Inventory Log Book is dedicated to resellers who want to keep accurate records and retain information for your online business.

You are my inspiration for producing this book and I'm honored to be a part of helping you manage and retain important information regarding your inventory, expenses, income, and listing goals.

HOW TO USE THIS BOOK

This Reseller Inventory Log Book will help you record, collect, and organize your information in an easy to use format.

Here are examples of information for you to fill in and write the details for your activities as a reseller.

Fill in the following information:

1. Listing Tracker - record monthly goals, record listing numbers for each week and month, space for notes

2. Inventory Tracker - listing name, cost, date of purchase, source, SKU, storage location, date listed, price sold, gross profit

3. Daily Sales - record daily/monthly sales, track: day, auction or buy it now, # of items, cost, item price, shipping, and total sales

4. Expense and Profit Track - record yearly total sales, total expenses, total profit, shipping fees, seller fees, yearly profit

LISTING TRACKER

| START DATE | | | NUMBER OF LISTING PER WEEK GOAL: | | | | | | |

MONTH	WEEK #	TOTAL ITEMS LISTED PER WEEK	ITEMS LISTED PER DAY						
			S	M	T	W	TH	F	S
	1								
	2								
	3								
	4								
	1								
	2								
	3								
	4								
	1								
	2								
	3								
	4								
	1								
	2								
	3								
	4								
	1								
	2								
	3								
	4								

NOTES	TOTAL LISTED FOR FIVE MONTHS

LISTING TRACKER

START DATE		NUMBER OF LISTING PER WEEK GOAL:	

MONTH	WEEK #	TOTAL ITEMS LISTED PER WEEK	ITEMS LISTED PER DAY						
			S	M	T	W	TH	F	S
	1								
	2								
	3								
	4								
	1								
	2								
	3								
	4								
	1								
	2								
	3								
	4								
	1								
	2								
	3								
	4								
	1								
	2								
	3								
	4								

NOTES	TOTAL LISTED FOR FIVE MONTHS

LISTING TRACKER

START DATE		NUMBER OF LISTING PER WEEK GOAL:	

MONTH	WEEK #	TOTAL ITEMS LISTED PER WEEK	ITEMS LISTED PER DAY						
			S	M	T	W	TH	F	S
	1								
	2								
	3								
	4								
	1								
	2								
	3								
	4								
	1								
	2								
	3								
	4								
	1								
	2								
	3								
	4								
	1								
	2								
	3								
	4								

NOTES	TOTAL LISTED FOR FIVE MONTHS

INVENTORY TRACKER

LISTING NAME	COST	DATE OF PURCHASED	SOURCE	SKU	STORAGE LOCATION	DATE LISTED	PRICE SOLD	GROSS PROFIT

INVENTORY TRACKER

LISTING NAME	COST	DATE OF PURCHASED	SOURCE	SKU	STORAGE LOCATION	DATE LISTED	PRICE SOLD	GROSS PROFIT

INVENTORY TRACKER

LISTING NAME	COST	DATE OF PURCHASED	SOURCE	SKU	STORAGE LOCATION	DATE LISTED	PRICE SOLD	GROSS PROFIT

INVENTORY TRACKER

LISTING NAME	COST	DATE OF PURCHASED	SOURCE	SKU	STORAGE LOCATION	DATE LISTED	PRICE SOLD	GROSS PROFIT

INVENTORY TRACKER

LISTING NAME	COST	DATE OF PURCHASED	SOURCE	SKU	STORAGE LOCATION	DATE LISTED	PRICE SOLD	GROSS PROFIT

INVENTORY TRACKER

LISTING NAME	COST	DATE OF PURCHASED	SOURCE	SKU	STORAGE LOCATION	DATE LISTED	PRICE SOLD	GROSS PROFIT

INVENTORY TRACKER

LISTING NAME	COST	DATE OF PURCHASED	SOURCE	SKU	STORAGE LOCATION	DATE LISTED	PRICE SOLD	GROSS PROFIT

INVENTORY TRACKER

LISTING NAME	COST	DATE OF PURCHASED	SOURCE	SKU	STORAGE LOCATION	DATE LISTED	PRICE SOLD	GROSS PROFIT

INVENTORY TRACKER

LISTING NAME	COST	DATE OF PURCHASED	SOURCE	SKU	STORAGE LOCATION	DATE LISTED	PRICE SOLD	GROSS PROFIT

INVENTORY TRACKER

LISTING NAME	COST	DATE OF PURCHASED	SOURCE	SKU	STORAGE LOCATION	DATE LISTED	PRICE SOLD	GROSS PROFIT

INVENTORY TRACKER

LISTING NAME	COST	DATE OF PURCHASED	SOURCE	SKU	STORAGE LOCATION	DATE LISTED	PRICE SOLD	GROSS PROFIT

INVENTORY TRACKER

LISTING NAME	COST	DATE OF PURCHASED	SOURCE	SKU	STORAGE LOCATION	DATE LISTED	PRICE SOLD	GROSS PROFIT

INVENTORY TRACKER

LISTING NAME	COST	DATE OF PURCHASED	SOURCE	SKU	STORAGE LOCATION	DATE LISTED	PRICE SOLD	GROSS PROFIT

INVENTORY TRACKER

LISTING NAME	COST	DATE OF PURCHASED	SOURCE	SKU	STORAGE LOCATION	DATE LISTED	PRICE SOLD	GROSS PROFIT

INVENTORY TRACKER

LISTING NAME	COST	DATE OF PURCHASED	SOURCE	SKU	STORAGE LOCATION	DATE LISTED	PRICE SOLD	GROSS PROFIT

INVENTORY TRACKER

LISTING NAME	COST	DATE OF PURCHASED	SOURCE	SKU	STORAGE LOCATION	DATE LISTED	PRICE SOLD	GROSS PROFIT

INVENTORY TRACKER

LISTING NAME	COST	DATE OF PURCHASED	SOURCE	SKU	STORAGE LOCATION	DATE LISTED	PRICE SOLD	GROSS PROFIT

INVENTORY TRACKER

LISTING NAME	COST	DATE OF PURCHASED	SOURCE	SKU	STORAGE LOCATION	DATE LISTED	PRICE SOLD	GROSS PROFIT

INVENTORY TRACKER

LISTING NAME	COST	DATE OF PURCHASED	SOURCE	SKU	STORAGE LOCATION	DATE LISTED	PRICE SOLD	GROSS PROFIT

INVENTORY TRACKER

LISTING NAME	COST	DATE OF PURCHASED	SOURCE	SKU	STORAGE LOCATION	DATE LISTED	PRICE SOLD	GROSS PROFIT

INVENTORY TRACKER

LISTING NAME	COST	DATE OF PURCHASED	SOURCE	SKU	STORAGE LOCATION	DATE LISTED	PRICE SOLD	GROSS PROFIT

INVENTORY TRACKER

LISTING NAME	COST	DATE OF PURCHASED	SOURCE	SKU	STORAGE LOCATION	DATE LISTED	PRICE SOLD	GROSS PROFIT

INVENTORY TRACKER

LISTING NAME	COST	DATE OF PURCHASED	SOURCE	SKU	STORAGE LOCATION	DATE LISTED	PRICE SOLD	GROSS PROFIT

INVENTORY TRACKER

LISTING NAME	COST	DATE OF PURCHASED	SOURCE	SKU	STORAGE LOCATION	DATE LISTED	PRICE SOLD	GROSS PROFIT

INVENTORY TRACKER

LISTING NAME	COST	DATE OF PURCHASED	SOURCE	SKU	STORAGE LOCATION	DATE LISTED	PRICE SOLD	GROSS PROFIT

INVENTORY TRACKER

LISTING NAME	COST	DATE OF PURCHASED	SOURCE	SKU	STORAGE LOCATION	DATE LISTED	PRICE SOLD	GROSS PROFIT

INVENTORY TRACKER

LISTING NAME	COST	DATE OF PURCHASED	SOURCE	SKU	STORAGE LOCATION	DATE LISTED	PRICE SOLD	GROSS PROFIT

INVENTORY TRACKER

LISTING NAME	COST	DATE OF PURCHASED	SOURCE	SKU	STORAGE LOCATION	DATE LISTED	PRICE SOLD	GROSS PROFIT

INVENTORY TRACKER

LISTING NAME	COST	DATE OF PURCHASED	SOURCE	SKU	STORAGE LOCATION	DATE LISTED	PRICE SOLD	GROSS PROFIT

INVENTORY TRACKER

LISTING NAME	COST	DATE OF PURCHASED	SOURCE	SKU	STORAGE LOCATION	DATE LISTED	PRICE SOLD	GROSS PROFIT

INVENTORY TRACKER

LISTING NAME	COST	DATE OF PURCHASED	SOURCE	SKU	STORAGE LOCATION	DATE LISTED	PRICE SOLD	GROSS PROFIT

INVENTORY TRACKER

LISTING NAME	COST	DATE OF PURCHASED	SOURCE	SKU	STORAGE LOCATION	DATE LISTED	PRICE SOLD	GROSS PROFIT

INVENTORY TRACKER

LISTING NAME	COST	DATE OF PURCHASED	SOURCE	SKU	STORAGE LOCATION	DATE LISTED	PRICE SOLD	GROSS PROFIT

INVENTORY TRACKER

LISTING NAME	COST	DATE OF PURCHASED	SOURCE	SKU	STORAGE LOCATION	DATE LISTED	PRICE SOLD	GROSS PROFIT

INVENTORY TRACKER

LISTING NAME	COST	DATE OF PURCHASED	SOURCE	SKU	STORAGE LOCATION	DATE LISTED	PRICE SOLD	GROSS PROFIT

INVENTORY TRACKER

LISTING NAME	COST	DATE OF PURCHASED	SOURCE	SKU	STORAGE LOCATION	DATE LISTED	PRICE SOLD	GROSS PROFIT

INVENTORY TRACKER

LISTING NAME	COST	DATE OF PURCHASED	SOURCE	SKU	STORAGE LOCATION	DATE LISTED	PRICE SOLD	GROSS PROFIT

INVENTORY TRACKER

LISTING NAME	COST	DATE OF PURCHASED	SOURCE	SKU	STORAGE LOCATION	DATE LISTED	PRICE SOLD	GROSS PROFIT

INVENTORY TRACKER

LISTING NAME	COST	DATE OF PURCHASED	SOURCE	SKU	STORAGE LOCATION	DATE LISTED	PRICE SOLD	GROSS PROFIT

INVENTORY TRACKER

LISTING NAME	COST	DATE OF PURCHASED	SOURCE	SKU	STORAGE LOCATION	DATE LISTED	PRICE SOLD	GROSS PROFIT

INVENTORY TRACKER

LISTING NAME	COST	DATE OF PURCHASED	SOURCE	SKU	STORAGE LOCATION	DATE LISTED	PRICE SOLD	GROSS PROFIT

INVENTORY TRACKER

LISTING NAME	COST	DATE OF PURCHASED	SOURCE	SKU	STORAGE LOCATION	DATE LISTED	PRICE SOLD	GROSS PROFIT

INVENTORY TRACKER

LISTING NAME	COST	DATE OF PURCHASED	SOURCE	SKU	STORAGE LOCATION	DATE LISTED	PRICE SOLD	GROSS PROFIT

INVENTORY TRACKER

LISTING NAME	COST	DATE OF PURCHASED	SOURCE	SKU	STORAGE LOCATION	DATE LISTED	PRICE SOLD	GROSS PROFIT

INVENTORY TRACKER

LISTING NAME	COST	DATE OF PURCHASED	SOURCE	SKU	STORAGE LOCATION	DATE LISTED	PRICE SOLD	GROSS PROFIT

INVENTORY TRACKER

LISTING NAME	COST	DATE OF PURCHASED	SOURCE	SKU	STORAGE LOCATION	DATE LISTED	PRICE SOLD	GROSS PROFIT

INVENTORY TRACKER

LISTING NAME	COST	DATE OF PURCHASED	SOURCE	SKU	STORAGE LOCATION	DATE LISTED	PRICE SOLD	GROSS PROFIT

INVENTORY TRACKER

LISTING NAME	COST	DATE OF PURCHASED	SOURCE	SKU	STORAGE LOCATION	DATE LISTED	PRICE SOLD	GROSS PROFIT

INVENTORY TRACKER

LISTING NAME	COST	DATE OF PURCHASED	SOURCE	SKU	STORAGE LOCATION	DATE LISTED	PRICE SOLD	GROSS PROFIT

INVENTORY TRACKER

LISTING NAME	COST	DATE OF PURCHASED	SOURCE	SKU	STORAGE LOCATION	DATE LISTED	PRICE SOLD	GROSS PROFIT

INVENTORY TRACKER

LISTING NAME	COST	DATE OF PURCHASED	SOURCE	SKU	STORAGE LOCATION	DATE LISTED	PRICE SOLD	GROSS PROFIT

INVENTORY TRACKER

LISTING NAME	COST	DATE OF PURCHASED	SOURCE	SKU	STORAGE LOCATION	DATE LISTED	PRICE SOLD	GROSS PROFIT

INVENTORY TRACKER

LISTING NAME	COST	DATE OF PURCHASED	SOURCE	SKU	STORAGE LOCATION	DATE LISTED	PRICE SOLD	GROSS PROFIT

INVENTORY TRACKER

LISTING NAME	COST	DATE OF PURCHASED	SOURCE	SKU	STORAGE LOCATION	DATE LISTED	PRICE SOLD	GROSS PROFIT

INVENTORY TRACKER

LISTING NAME	COST	DATE OF PURCHASED	SOURCE	SKU	STORAGE LOCATION	DATE LISTED	PRICE SOLD	GROSS PROFIT

INVENTORY TRACKER

LISTING NAME	COST	DATE OF PURCHASED	SOURCE	SKU	STORAGE LOCATION	DATE LISTED	PRICE SOLD	GROSS PROFIT

INVENTORY TRACKER

LISTING NAME	COST	DATE OF PURCHASED	SOURCE	SKU	STORAGE LOCATION	DATE LISTED	PRICE SOLD	GROSS PROFIT

INVENTORY TRACKER

LISTING NAME	COST	DATE OF PURCHASED	SOURCE	SKU	STORAGE LOCATION	DATE LISTED	PRICE SOLD	GROSS PROFIT

INVENTORY TRACKER

LISTING NAME	COST	DATE OF PURCHASED	SOURCE	SKU	STORAGE LOCATION	DATE LISTED	PRICE SOLD	GROSS PROFIT

INVENTORY TRACKER

LISTING NAME	COST	DATE OF PURCHASED	SOURCE	SKU	STORAGE LOCATION	DATE LISTED	PRICE SOLD	GROSS PROFIT

INVENTORY TRACKER

LISTING NAME	COST	DATE OF PURCHASED	SOURCE	SKU	STORAGE LOCATION	DATE LISTED	PRICE SOLD	GROSS PROFIT

INVENTORY TRACKER

LISTING NAME	COST	DATE OF PURCHASED	SOURCE	SKU	STORAGE LOCATION	DATE LISTED	PRICE SOLD	GROSS PROFIT

INVENTORY TRACKER

LISTING NAME	COST	DATE OF PURCHASED	SOURCE	SKU	STORAGE LOCATION	DATE LISTED	PRICE SOLD	GROSS PROFIT

INVENTORY TRACKER

LISTING NAME	COST	DATE OF PURCHASED	SOURCE	SKU	STORAGE LOCATION	DATE LISTED	PRICE SOLD	GROSS PROFIT

INVENTORY TRACKER

LISTING NAME	COST	DATE OF PURCHASED	SOURCE	SKU	STORAGE LOCATION	DATE LISTED	PRICE SOLD	GROSS PROFIT

DAILY SALES
JANUARY

WEEKDAY	DATE	AUCTIONS	BUY IT NOW	# OF ITEMS	COST	ITEM PRICE	SHIPPING	TOTAL SALES
	1							
	2							
	3							
	4							
	5							
	6							
	7							
	8							
	9							
	10							
	11							
	12							
	13							
	14							
	15							
	16							
	17							
	18							
	19							
	20							
	21							
	22							
	23							
	24							
	25							
	26							
	27							
	28							
	29							
	30							
	31							
		AVERAGE						
		TOTAL						

DAILY SALES
FEBRUARY

WEEKDAY	DATE	AUCTIONS	BUY IT NOW	# OF ITEMS	COST	ITEM PRICE	SHIPPING	TOTAL SALES
	1							
	2							
	3							
	4							
	5							
	6							
	7							
	8							
	9							
	10							
	11							
	12							
	13							
	14							
	15							
	16							
	17							
	18							
	19							
	20							
	21							
	22							
	23							
	24							
	25							
	26							
	27							
	28							
	29							
	30							
	31							
		AVERAGE						
		TOTAL						

DAILY SALES
MARCH

WEEKDAY	DATE	AUCTIONS	BUY IT NOW	# OF ITEMS	COST	ITEM PRICE	SHIPPING	TOTAL SALES
	1							
	2							
	3							
	4							
	5							
	6							
	7							
	8							
	9							
	10							
	11							
	12							
	13							
	14							
	15							
	16							
	17							
	18							
	19							
	20							
	21							
	22							
	23							
	24							
	25							
	26							
	27							
	28							
	29							
	30							
	31							
		AVERAGE						
		TOTAL						

DAILY SALES
APRIL

WEEKDAY	DATE	AUCTIONS	BUY IT NOW	# OF ITEMS	COST	ITEM PRICE	SHIPPING	TOTAL SALES
	1							
	2							
	3							
	4							
	5							
	6							
	7							
	8							
	9							
	10							
	11							
	12							
	13							
	14							
	15							
	16							
	17							
	18							
	19							
	20							
	21							
	22							
	23							
	24							
	25							
	26							
	27							
	28							
	29							
	30							
	31							
		AVERAGE						
		TOTAL						

DAILY SALES
MAY

WEEKDAY	DATE	AUCTIONS	BUY IT NOW	# OF ITEMS	COST	ITEM PRICE	SHIPPING	TOTAL SALES
	1							
	2							
	3							
	4							
	5							
	6							
	7							
	8							
	9							
	10							
	11							
	12							
	13							
	14							
	15							
	16							
	17							
	18							
	19							
	20							
	21							
	22							
	23							
	24							
	25							
	26							
	27							
	28							
	29							
	30							
	31							
		AVERAGE						
		TOTAL						

DAILY SALES
JUNE

WEEKDAY	DATE	AUCTIONS	BUY IT NOW	# OF ITEMS	COST	ITEM PRICE	SHIPPING	TOTAL SALES
	1							
	2							
	3							
	4							
	5							
	6							
	7							
	8							
	9							
	10							
	11							
	12							
	13							
	14							
	15							
	16							
	17							
	18							
	19							
	20							
	21							
	22							
	23							
	24							
	25							
	26							
	27							
	28							
	29							
	30							
	31							
		AVERAGE						
		TOTAL						

DAILY SALES
JULY

WEEKDAY	DATE	AUCTIONS	BUY IT NOW	# OF ITEMS	COST	ITEM PRICE	SHIPPING	TOTAL SALES
	1							
	2							
	3							
	4							
	5							
	6							
	7							
	8							
	9							
	10							
	11							
	12							
	13							
	14							
	15							
	16							
	17							
	18							
	19							
	20							
	21							
	22							
	23							
	24							
	25							
	26							
	27							
	28							
	29							
	30							
	31							
		AVERAGE						
		TOTAL						

DAILY SALES
AUGUST

WEEKDAY	DATE	AUCTIONS	BUY IT NOW	# OF ITEMS	COST	ITEM PRICE	SHIPPING	TOTAL SALES
	1							
	2							
	3							
	4							
	5							
	6							
	7							
	8							
	9							
	10							
	11							
	12							
	13							
	14							
	15							
	16							
	17							
	18							
	19							
	20							
	21							
	22							
	23							
	24							
	25							
	26							
	27							
	28							
	29							
	30							
	31							
		AVERAGE						
		TOTAL						

DAILY SALES
SEPTEMBER

WEEKDAY	DATE	AUCTIONS	BUY IT NOW	# OF ITEMS	COST	ITEM PRICE	SHIPPING	TOTAL SALES
	1							
	2							
	3							
	4							
	5							
	6							
	7							
	8							
	9							
	10							
	11							
	12							
	13							
	14							
	15							
	16							
	17							
	18							
	19							
	20							
	21							
	22							
	23							
	24							
	25							
	26							
	27							
	28							
	29							
	30							
	31							
	AVERAGE							
	TOTAL							

DAILY SALES
OCTOBER

WEEKDAY	DATE	AUCTIONS	BUY IT NOW	# OF ITEMS	COST	ITEM PRICE	SHIPPING	TOTAL SALES
	1							
	2							
	3							
	4							
	5							
	6							
	7							
	8							
	9							
	10							
	11							
	12							
	13							
	14							
	15							
	16							
	17							
	18							
	19							
	20							
	21							
	22							
	23							
	24							
	25							
	26							
	27							
	28							
	29							
	30							
	31							
		AVERAGE						
		TOTAL						

DAILY SALES
NOVEMBER

WEEKDAY	DATE	AUCTIONS	BUY IT NOW	# OF ITEMS	COST	ITEM PRICE	SHIPPING	TOTAL SALES
	1							
	2							
	3							
	4							
	5							
	6							
	7							
	8							
	9							
	10							
	11							
	12							
	13							
	14							
	15							
	16							
	17							
	18							
	19							
	20							
	21							
	22							
	23							
	24							
	25							
	26							
	27							
	28							
	29							
	30							
	31							
		AVERAGE						
		TOTAL						

DAILY SALES
DECEMBER

WEEKDAY	DATE	AUCTIONS	BUY IT NOW	# OF ITEMS	COST	ITEM PRICE	SHIPPING	TOTAL SALES
	1							
	2							
	3							
	4							
	5							
	6							
	7							
	8							
	9							
	10							
	11							
	12							
	13							
	14							
	15							
	16							
	17							
	18							
	19							
	20							
	21							
	22							
	23							
	24							
	25							
	26							
	27							
	28							
	29							
	30							
	31							
		AVERAGE						
		TOTAL						

EXPENSE AND PROFIT TRACKER

MONTH	TOTAL SALES		TOTAL SPENT		TOTAL PROFIT
JANUARY		-		=	
FEBRUARY		-		=	
MARCH		-		=	
APRIL		-		=	
MAY		-		=	
JUNE		-		=	
JULY		-		=	
AUGUST		-		=	
SEPTEMBER		-		=	
OCTOBER		-		=	
NOVEMBER		-		=	
DECEMBER		-		=	
TOTAL		-		=	

MONTH	SHIPPING FEES		SELLING FEES		TOTAL EXPENSES
JANUARY		+		=	
FEBRUARY		+		=	
MARCH		+		=	
APRIL		+		=	
MAY		+		=	
JUNE		+		=	
JULY		+		=	
AUGUST		+		=	
SEPTEMBER		+		=	
OCTOBER		+		=	
NOVEMBER		+		=	
DECEMBER		+		=	
TOTAL		+		=	

TOTAL SALES		TOTAL EXPENSES		SHIPPING EXPENSES	
SELLER FEES		OTHER EXPENSES		YEARLY PROFIT	

MILEAGE TRACKER

DATE	BUSINESS PURPOSE	ODOMETER START	ODOMETER END	TOTAL MILES
			RUNNING TOTAL	

MILEAGE TRACKER

DATE	BUSINESS PURPOSE	ODOMETER START	ODOMETER END	TOTAL MILES
			RUNNING TOTAL	

MILEAGE TRACKER

DATE	BUSINESS PURPOSE	ODOMETER START	ODOMETER END	TOTAL MILES
			RUNNING TOTAL	

MILEAGE TRACKER

DATE	BUSINESS PURPOSE	ODOMETER START	ODOMETER END	TOTAL MILES
			RUNNING TOTAL	

MILEAGE TRACKER

DATE	BUSINESS PURPOSE	ODOMETER START	ODOMETER END	TOTAL MILES
			RUNNING TOTAL	

MILEAGE TRACKER

DATE	BUSINESS PURPOSE	ODOMETER START	ODOMETER END	TOTAL MILES
			RUNNING TOTAL	

MILEAGE TRACKER

DATE	BUSINESS PURPOSE	ODOMETER START	ODOMETER END	TOTAL MILES
			RUNNING TOTAL	

MILEAGE TRACKER

DATE	BUSINESS PURPOSE	ODOMETER START	ODOMETER END	TOTAL MILES
			RUNNING TOTAL	

MILEAGE TRACKER

DATE	BUSINESS PURPOSE	ODOMETER START	ODOMETER END	TOTAL MILES
			RUNNING TOTAL	

MILEAGE TRACKER

DATE	BUSINESS PURPOSE	ODOMETER START	ODOMETER END	TOTAL MILES
				RUNNING TOTAL

MILEAGE TRACKER

DATE	BUSINESS PURPOSE	ODOMETER START	ODOMETER END	TOTAL MILES
			RUNNING TOTAL	

MILEAGE TRACKER

DATE	BUSINESS PURPOSE	ODOMETER START	ODOMETER END	TOTAL MILES
			RUNNING TOTAL	

www.ingramcontent.com/pod-product-compliance
Lightning Source LLC
Chambersburg PA
CBHW081157070526
44583CB00021B/2877